Know About
Subhash chandra Bose

KNOW ABOUT SUBHASH CHANDRA BOSE

ALL RIGHTS RESERVED. No part of this book may be reproduced in a retrieval system or transmitted in any form or by any means electronics, mechanical, photocopying, recording and or without permission of the publisher.

Published by

MAPLE PRESS PRIVATE LIMITED
office: A-63, Sector 58, Noida 201301, U.P., India
phone: +91 120 455 3581, 455 3583
email: info@maplepress.co.in
website: www.maplepress.co.in

Reprinted in 2019

ISBN: 978-93-50334-14-0

Contents

Preface 4
1. Birth 6
2. Early Years of Shaping Up 9
3. Effect of Deshbandhu 12
4. Impression on Deshbandhu 16
5. Arrest of Bose 19
6. Release of Bose 22
7. Seeds of Socialism 25
8. The Problem of Illiteracy 28
9. Hindi- The National Language 31
10. Freedom 35
11. The Revolutionary Motto -Poorna Swaraj 39
12. Bose's Meeting with Gandhiji 42
13. Bose's deteriorating health and escape to Europe 45
14. Bose's Educational Philosophy 48
15. Originality of Thought 51
16. End of Civil Disobedience 54
17. The World Scene 57
18. Bose: The Congress President 60
19. Period of Struggle and Escape 63
20. Plan of Escape 66
21. Azad Hind Fauj 69
22. Bose: The INA Chief 72
23. Victory and Defeat of INA 74
24. Bose's Life Events in Chronology 77

Preface

Subhash Chandra Bose was a revolutionary in the pre-independence era who actively participated in the freedom struggle of India. Known as Netaji for his excellent leadership skills, he followed a groundbreaking path and put all his efforts to free India from the clutches of Britishers.

Bose led the Indian National Army during the 1920s and 1930s and went on to become the president of the Indian National Congress from 1937 to 1939. He is considered to be a legendary figure in the history of Indian Independence Struggle and played a vital role in the freedom struggle.

He gave up all his personal desires and tirelessly worked towards his one goal: to free his country from the bonds of slavery at the hands of the British. His methods and approaches were quite extraordinary and unacceptable by the revolutionaries of his time but his burning patriotism for his country was the sole factor that guided him in all his endeavours. He was a true patriot who was ready to lay down his life for his country.

By reading this book, the readers will get an insight into the life of Subhash Chandra Bose. Students can learn from his failures, get motivated by his achievements and develop an unending love and respect for their country.

CHAPTER 1
Birth

Subhash Chandra Bose was born on January 23, 1897, in Cuttack as the ninth child among fourteen children of Janakinath Bose, an advocate and Prabhavari Devi, a pure and God-fearing lady. In his biography, Subhash Chandra Bose has written that he used to have a very low opinion about himself. He considered himself as nothing. In his childhood, he desired for the attention and closeness of his parents but he did not get it because his family was very big.

He was admitted to the protestant European school in Cuttack. This school had a good reputation. He learnt discipline in the school. Moreover, he got attracted towards social service and secret societies that were working from Bengal.

At the age of fifteen, Bose read the speeches and writings of Swami Vivekananda. He became greatly interested in the teachings of Sri Ramakrishna Paramahansa too.

This influence lasted till the very end of his life. In his mind these influences led to a conflict between becoming a man of action to free India and becoming a religious person. He resolved this problem by choosing the ideology of selfless service towards Mother India.

As he grew up, he realised that his view differed from his friends. That could be the reason why he did not have any complaints when he left school in the year 1909.

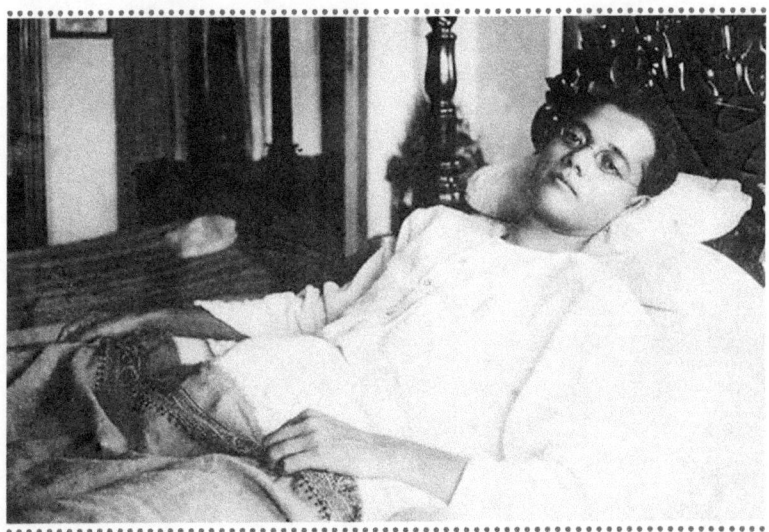

Then he took admission in the Revenasha Collegiate School. There he observed an emotional change in himself. The atmosphere of the school was completely Indian. That atmosphere slowly put a new confidence in him. In his school, he was known as a serious and reserved boy. He was never interested in sports.

However, he was interested with the visits of the 'sadhus' and pilgrims to 'Jagannath Puri', the famous holy place near his homeland.

CHAPTER 2
Early Years of Shaping Up

After finishing school, Bose took admission in Presidency College, Calcutta. He chose philosophy as his subject and went in search of a Guru in 1914.

But he faced disappointment in his search as he was unable to find a Guru and so he changed his mind to other interests. In his college he started a debating club. He said that India would need great debaters and parliamentarians in her coming struggle for independence.

He tried to promote quick thinking and independence among his co-students. The first turning point in his life came when he was expelled from his college for taking a leading part in beating up an English Professor of his college. He had an ill-feeling towards racial order and it was this that led to this fight. His father refused to admit him in any other college. Bose was readmitted to the same University the following year.

And later on, there were no problems with his education and he took his degree with a First Class Honours in Philosophy.

India was passing through hard times in those years and Bose's father did not want his young son to be affected by it. He wanted him to appear in the ICS examinations. From inside, Bose was a true nationalist but he also wanted to go to England for higher studies. Ultimately, he decided to go to England. So his father sent him to England to compete in the ICS examination.

In England, he first stayed with his brother. Later, with the help of his friends and a college dean Mr. Redave, he got admission in Cambridge. He enjoyed his stay in England and the independence people enjoyed over there. But he always remembered that his own country was still under the British rule.

Bose qualified the ICS exam in 1920 and secured a high place. The family built high hopes on their brilliant son. Subhash Chandra Bose wanted to remain loyal to the nation as well as to the family. It was at that time that Mahatma Gandhi had started his Non-Cooperation Movement and requested all patriots to give away all the British titles granted to them personally.

The Mahatma's request attracted Bose so much that he resigned from the ICS and returned to India in 1921 to place himself in his hands. He informed about this decision to his family through a letter.

CHAPTER 3
Effect of Deshbandhu

Subhash Chandra went to Mumbai to meet Gandhiji. Gandhiji was of the view that non-violence was the only feasible approach for freedom struggle. Bose never agreed with his view. He realised that the non-violence movement undertaken by Gandhiji was just a program for national freedom. He impressed Gandhiji with his revolutionary views to such an extent that he sent this young man to work under the guidance of Deshbandhu Chittaranjan Das.

At that time, Deshbandhu was the most famous lawyer of Bengal. He always used to help the freedom fighters with money and maintained a strong relationship with them. He always wanted that educated middle class nationalists should help the villagers by creating awareness among the people. He actively participated in the non-cooperation movement and gave up all his luxuries in order to become a part of the freedom struggle of India. In 1921, Bose organised a boycott of the celebrations used to mark the Prince of Wales' visit to India. This led to his imprisonment.

In April 1924, Bose was elected as the Chief Executive Officer of the newly formed Calcutta Corporation.

The political environment of the nation was getting tensed day by day and by the end of the year there was trouble in the nation due to the Non-Cooperation Movement launched by Gandhiji. Calcutta was the center of this movement. The Non-Cooperation Movement and the Khilafat Movement started almost around the same time. The British government was confused. Though the aim of abolishing the British rule was no way near but still nationalist forces were so confident that Gandhiji gave a warning to the new viceroy that if the ruling government did not change its approach then people would stop paying the taxes. Such preparations were made all over the nation so that a sudden movement could be launched. The international situation was also favourable for Indian demands. Leaders like Deshbandhu Das and Subhash Chandra Bose were in jail with their followers from the beginning of December 1921.

At the beginning of 1921, Congress gained great popularity in Bengal and Bose played an important role in this. The new constitution provided by Gandhiji helped the entry of a large number of people in the party. The tricolour was now regarded as the national flag. Everywhere there were similar slogans, khadi dresses, policies and same ideologies. In this tensed situation of Bengal, the person whom Deshbandhu gave most of the responsibility was none other than Bose. This 24-year-old young boy was very much popular among the people for his educational qualifications and he also proved that he was not selfish by rejecting the post offered in the civil service.

He was the strength behind the institutions like the R.S.S and other nationalist educational institutions. This proved him to be an able leader and after this he became responsible for the works of the national press. On the other hand, acting as a member of South Calcutta Service Committee he took part in the social upliftment of the south Calcutta region.

CHAPTER 4
Impression on Deshbandhu

The year 1922 started off with a blurred vision of the revolutionaries and little excitement regarding the political scenario of the country. The Viceroy took the offer of settlement back. Gandhiji warned the British about the non-payment of tax movement from Bardoli, Gujarat. Then the incidence of Chauri-Chaura happened in Gorakhpur, when the angry villagers protested against the increased price of the meat and were beaten back by

the police. As a result, the protestors set the police station on fire, killing more than a score of policemen. Gandhiji was shocked by the incident and disappointed at the violence created by the protestors. Therefore, he halted the Non-Cooperation movement. At that time Bose was in jail with Deshbandhu. This news of the delay of the movement angered and depressed them. The sad situation disappointed the Congress members. Viceroy studied the situation and took advantage, he took severe action against Gandhiji and this led to a long-term jail sentence for him on the charges of disloyalty towards the state.

In September 1922, the northern districts of Bengal faced a severe flood situation. The Congress workers provided help to the needy at the right time. Bose was the head of the first batch of the rescue group. He worked for days and nights for six weeks and made every effort to save the people of the northern Bengal. His work was so valuable that it helped the Congress party to become popular among the crowds.

In the year 1922, two incidents occurred, which made an excellent impression of Bose on Deshbandhu. The first one was the Lahore meeting of the All India Trade Union Congress in which Deshbandhu acted as a president. It was at this meeting that Deshbandhu declared in clear words that the freedom for which they were fighting was for the people who constituted 98 percent of the Indian population. In a similar manner, Bose began the Indian

Labour Movement and by following into the wise man's footsteps, he not only became All India Trade Union Congress's president but also got the top position of Tata Iron and Steel Labour Association.

The second incident was the Young Men's Conference that was organised in Kolkata and very soon young Bose became the leader of this body. At the end of the ten years, India's youth movement became an influential force with Jawaharlal Nehru and Subhash Chandra Bose as its leaders. A meeting of All India Congress Committee was held in Kolkata in 1922 and Deshbandhu was the President of the meeting. At this meeting both the groups debated on many topics. In the Gaya Congress the proposal of Deshbandhu was not accepted and due to this, his position as the president began to shake.

CHAPTER 5
Arrest of Bose

Finally the time came when the plan of Congress was to be finalised for the coming year. At that time, Motilal Nehru surprised everyone by declaring that he was forming a new party called the 'Swaraj Party'. Deshbandhu was against the plan and so he resigned from his position. Bose has written that Swarajwadis were defeated before, but they were always devoted and committed to freedom struggle and found a new way ahead.

After the end of the Non-cooperation movement and Khilafat movement, Deshbandhu had realised that without the unity of the Hindus and Muslims the struggle for freedom was not possible. So he invited major political leaders and there was an agreement signed between the two communities, which later became popular as 'the Bengal Pact'. Bose fully supported this pact.

Deshbandhu appointed Bose as the new authority head of the Kolkata Municipal Corporation. The Kolkata Municipal Corporation came out with an English journal whose editor was one of the friends of Bose. This journal published a photograph of Bose in which he was being beaten by the police while leading a congress procession. This gave a chance to the British government to act against Bose. Bose was arrested as a suspected dangerous terrorist. Reacting on this incident, Deshbandhu said that the only crime of Bose was his love for the nation.

Bose spent four long years in jail. He was shifted from the Alipore jail to the great fort of Mandalay in Burma. However, there is no police record which proves that Bose actively took part in the revolutionary violence. He liked the spirit of the young revolutionaries. The government was pretty sure that Bose provided shelter to the revolutionaries.

This was the period of intense ups and downs in Bengal. Deshbandhu's death on 6th June 1925 came as a major shock to the leading revolutionaries. He died due to long illness. Bose acknowledged later that Deshbandhu was a fearless man who had the capability to change the face of India through his skills and courage. The jail authorities in Mandalay were very cruel and thus, Bose and the other prisoners were left with no other alternative but to go on a hunger strike that started from February 18, 1926. On the eighth day of the strike the authorities gave them food forcefully. This action made the whole nation worry about the state of the prisoners. Due to this strike Bose lost a lot of weight. The results of this strike lifted his confidence greatly. But the condition of Bose kept on getting worse day by day. The medical examination disclosed that he was ill due to T.B. and he could recover only in some hilly region. The government agreed to send him to Almora.

CHAPTER 6
Release of Bose

He boarded the steamer that was going to Kolkata. The doctors said that his health was in a very bad condition. This was the reason for which he was unconditionally released. He went to Shillong and rested there for five months and then returned to active politics. As he made a comeback, he was elected as the president of the Bengal Congress Committee. This opened a new chapter in his life.

Anti-British feelings were spreading in the nation and Indians wanted some good leaders to run their country. Noticing that restlessness was spreading, the British Government appointed a commission to report on the political happenings, under the leadership of Sir John Simon in 1928. There was no single Indian member in this commission and all the political parties decided to boycott the commission when it planned to visit the major cities of India.

The National Muslim League in its Kolkata meeting passed a resolution for the Hindu-Muslim unity and decided to reject the Simon Commission. Bose was of the opinion that this was possible because Muslim leaders like Jinnah and Ali brothers were present over there.

On February 3, 1928, Simon Commission came to India and Congress was successful in its 'bandh' all over the country. Bose wanted to launch the movement on a large scale. He believed that if the Congress Working Committee acted in a brave manner then this movement could have been started two years earlier.

On the day of the arrival of Simon Commission there were mass protests in Kolkata and Bengal in order to ban the use of foreign clothes. Bose played a major role in these protests. The echoes of these protests could be heard all over the nation and the slogans of 'Simon Go Back' could be heard everywhere. The most surprising thing in this whole act was the labour class who took part in this movement in huge numbers. The young people were ahead everywhere and were always prepared to fight. Jawaharlal Nehru and Bose were invited to participate in many protest meetings.

The annual Congress meet was planned at the end of December 1928 in Kolkata. Before this the students supporting the left front organised a regional student summit in September 1928. At this meeting only the birth of Bengal students' union took place.

CHAPTER 7
Seeds of Socialism

The writings, speeches and talks of Netaji often displayed his understanding of social and economic problems of India. These documents are considered to be a special study material in social modernisation even today.

Bose's main aim was to sow the seeds of socialism in India. He declared, at the Haripura Congress Session in 1938, that poverty, illiteracy and diseases would be removed with the help of socialism. To spread his socialistic ideals, Bose wanted a National Planning Commission. Even while leading an armed struggle for India's freedom, he had formed a separate department for his Army to make the staff know about their ideologies.

He always followed three aims. The aims were: to erase poverty and unemployment, fight against diseases and illiteracy and to build a strong national defense system.

To erase poverty and unemployment, he stated that the State should give importance to modern agricultural and industrial practices. He realised that developing the

agricultural field and the home industry would provide an increase in India's economics.

He always suggested the end of the 'zamindari' system, radical land reforms, promotion of agricultural loans and to develop co-operative movement, increasing agricultural production, scientific methods, widespread industrial development plan under State control and at the same time, starting of cottage industries in the necessary fields and all other required points in India's fight against poverty and unemployment.

In a speech to the students of Tokyo Imperial University in November 1944, he said that, to fight against the problems of Indians one should follow Indian methods under Indian environment and also it should suit Indian people. To gain it we need to study about the workings of other countries and apply it to our own.

CHAPTER 8
The Problem of Illiteracy

The objective of Bose's socialistic thoughts was to improve the condition of the masses of India, whom he called as 'have-nots' and even today these people are a part of the majority of India's population. One of the major achievements of the Congress's Kolkata meeting was the

marching of labourers under the leadership of leftists, communists and socialist congress leaders. Bose took active part in this meeting. In 1928, he announced that the Gandhian ideology and Pondicherry ideology were producing two different effects. He said that they want every person to take active part in the making of the modern India and everyone must shape themselves in accordance with the prevailing conditions. Netaji Bose was of the view that illiteracy was one of the greatest defects of the Indian society and the most burdensome difficulty in the path of the development of the masses. He had a long background of social service and the important part of it was to erase illiteracy from the face of India. Even when he was a school student he was attached to a Night School of Krishnanagar where students from poor families received an education. At this point of time, Subhash Chandra Bose was under the influence of Swami Vivekananda who was the shining hero of mass education. Bose always gave education to the illiterate masses in order to lift them up from the grip of ignorance. Thus, even when he was imprisoned in Mandalay, he wrote in an undated letter to Bhupendra Nath Banerjee asking him to open a school for children of the lower classes like cobblers and sweepers.

Subhash Chandra Bose's fight against illiteracy was based on the unrecognised right to education for all classes of people and which was needed for the formation of a socialist state in India. Speaking at the University

Institute Hall in November 1927 at the All Bengal Youth Conference, Subhash Chandra Bose stated that the lack of food, clothing and education were the three major needs of the Indian people. Thus, to satisfy these needs one must act in the villages and from the basic level. Unfortunately, his mission to eradicate illiteracy is still not accomplished as there are thousands of illiterate people roaming around the streets of our country even today.

CHAPTER 9
Hindi - The National Language

Subhash Chandra Bose always puts stress on self-dependence. But he also said that in order to develop a nation one needs to make the base strong. Therefore, it is important to provide help during the initial phase and later the community would definitely come forward and show the desire to stand up on their feet.

Subhash Chandra Bose expressed his views by saying that national education would not be complete if one is not given knowledge of patriotism and nationalism. Every child from its birth must be taught to love their country and fulfill their duty towards the development of their country all through their life.

The Provisional Government adhered to the concept of national education by giving knowledge about patriotism and by rising national pride. The goal of Bose was to shape young minds with scientific knowledge raising them above the theories of orthodox superstitions. Bose's statement at the Maharashtra Provincial Conference at Poona on

May 5, 1928 was that the cure for backward life was to get knowledge about secular and scientific education.

In the 'Rastra Bhasha Sammelan', he addressed the audiences in Hindi. The problem of the national language continues to trouble India even today. There have been language riots in South India where people dislike Hindi. A uniform national language policy is yet to be formed in order to erase the language difference that blocks national unity.

In his speech delivered as the Chairman of the Reception Committee, 'Rastra Bhasha Sammelan', on December, 28, 1928, Subhash Chandra Bose expressed his liking for the Hindi language. He also talked with the Bengalis who were opposed to the idea of 'Hindi being the national language of India'. He recalled the contribution of famous Bengalis to the Hindi literature and journalism particularly that of Bhudev Mukherjee, Navin Chandra Roy and Amiya Chakroborty. Subhash Chandra Bose who was a believer in the provincial autonomy said that to exchange ideas with people one must know the common Hindustani language. He also remarked, "The day is not distant when Hindi will be the national language of the 'Swadhin Bharat.'" His words have been forgotten by the citizens of independent India who feel ashamed to

converse in their national language and do not give it the importance and respect that it deserves. No matter how many languages we know, our national language shall always remain to be more than a mere set of grammatical rules and a process of conversation. It reflects our identity, our culture and our heritage. You may choose any other language and fall in love with it but not at the cost of disregarding and condemning the language that forms an integral part of your social being.

CHAPTER 10
Freedom

Subhash Chandra Bose was an expert in Sanskrit but he did not support Sanskrit as the national language of India. The reason was that, he did not consider it as a practicable language in the days of the national movement. With its complicated structure and grammar, it was difficult to comprehend the language and become well-versed in it. Also, at that time, it was important for people of different

areas to come under one banner for the struggle against the British Empire.

Therefore, he supported the stand of making Hindi as the national language since it was an easy-to-learn language and within the reach of the common man. Bose also inspired women to unite and fight for their rights and for the freedom of the nation.

The British studied the situation as very dangerous for the well-being of the government. In the last days of 1928, the revolutionaries, associated with the Hindustan Socialist Republican Army, shot a police officer. Another incident occurred in April 1929, when two young revolutionaries threw a tear gas bomb in the state assembly of Delhi and distributed a notice that an armed revolution against the British was about to start. On this ground the British government started arresting the suspected revolutionaries and in July 1929, the Lahore All India Conspiracy Case was started.

Bhagat Singh was the active leader of North India's revolutionaries and his organisation received a huge support from the people. Bhagat Singh became a hero for the masses. Many songs were composed on him and the youth throughout the country made him their ideal. He became a symbol of bravery with an aim to free India.

Bhagat Singh was born in a Sikh family of farmers in the village of Banga of Layalpur district of Punjab (now in Pakistan) on September 27, 1907. Bhagat Singh's father

Kishen Singh and his uncle Ajit Singh were members of the Ghadar party founded in the U.S. in the early years of the 20th century to route the British rule in India. Both were jailed for anti-British activities. 22 cases were registered against Ajit Singh that led him to escape to

Iran. From there, he visited many countries like Turkey, Austria, Germany and finally Brazil to escape the punishment of becoming a prisoner in the 'Black Water' (Kalapani) prison. The British government tried to keep away the communist party from the main revolution but the opposite happened. Subhash Chandra Bose along with the other leftist leaders expressed sympathy for the revolutionaries who were in the Lahore jail.

CHAPTER 11
The Revolutionary Motto - Poorna Swaraj

Jawaharlal Nehru and Gandhiji presided the Lahore meeting of the congress. They forwarded the proposal of 'Total Freedom' or 'Poorna Swaraj'. Subhash Chandra Bose wanted to gain complete freedom for India as early as possible. On the other hand, the Congress Committee wanted it in accordance with the British dominance. Jawaharlal Nehru and other younger leaders were supporting Subhash Chandra Bose. Thus, the result was that the Congress had to adopt 'Poorna Swaraj' (complete freedom) as its motto. This proposal was approved by all the members of the Congress.

After his arrival in Kolkata he was arrested and was sentenced to heavy imprisonment for one year, which was later reduced to nine months.

Gandhiji was then preparing for his 'Satyagraha' for salt. There were huge differences between Bose and him. When Subhash Chandra Bose was in jail, India was at the point of a fierce freedom struggle.

The year 1930 was a stormy year for the Indian freedom struggle. Gandhiji was the big leader of the nation. He started a new revolution by suggesting that 26th January should be celebrated as the Independence Day. After 1930, this day was dedicated towards the freedom of the motherland.

While starting the salt movement, Gandhiji announced that under his leadership this movement would be started by a few chosen leaders. Then they all will march towards Dandi. He went with the other leaders and when they reached the shore, they broke the salt law along with millions of Indians. The police lathi charged on men in a cruel manner. The foreign journalists who were the eyewitness of this whole action were greatly shocked by this behaviour.

Subhash Chandra Bose was elected as the mayor of Kolkata Municipal Corporation on August 22, 1930. On the 23rd of the next month he was released from jail and took the oath as the mayor of Kolkata.

On the eve of the 'Independence Day' of the year 1931, Subhash Chandra Bose was leading the largest rally of people to the Kolkata ground for hoisting the national flag. The British authorities were absolutely against it and ensured that the flag hoisting does not takes place by attacking the rally and severely injuring the people. Subhash Chandra Bose was also beaten with sticks and was later taken to the Lalbazaar police station. He was kept under arrest for 24 hours without any food or medicines. All his clothes were wet with blood. The next day when he was presented before the judge of the chief presidency he was in the same torn clothes. The 'satyagrahis' did not protect themselves from the cruelty of police. This was the reason why Subhash Chandra Bose didn't protect him and was sentenced to a six months severe imprisonment.

CHAPTER 12
Bose's Meeting with Gandhiji

The Congress leaders and the British government signed an agreement on March 4 after the Non-Cooperation Movement came to an end. Bose was informed about this in jail and he did not approve of it. He was not satisfied with the role played by Jawaharlal Nehru and later wrote that there was a huge responsibility on the shoulders of Jawaharlal Nehru and it was not because he was the Congress president at that time but also because he was

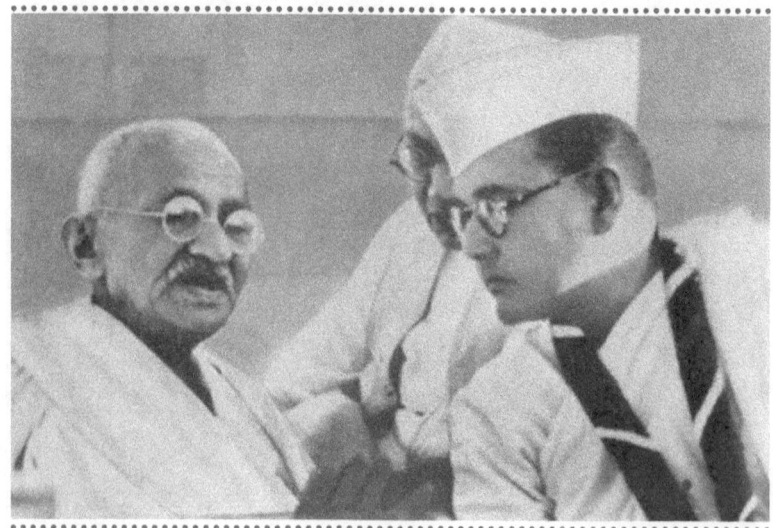

the only person who was expected to understand their condition. Bhagat Singh's sacrifice and the inability of the Congress leaders to save his life angered Bose.

Immediately, after getting released from jail, he went to Mumbai to meet Gandhiji. He told Gandhiji that he totally agreed with Jawaharlal Nehru that in comparison to the returns of the Gandhi-Irwin pact, the number of difficulties that Congress workers faced during the last year were increased. Their talk lasted for two days but he was unable to satisfy Gandhiji on this issue. The main point of discussion between both of them was - the question of the release of all political prisoners. According to Bose around 800 prisoners of Bengal had not been released though it was in the agreement. They all were imprisoned without any reason and still retained.

Gandhiji's opinion was that these prisoners did not take the oath of non-violence and hence didn't come

under the category of Congress Satyagrahis. At the end of March 1931, a special meeting of the Indian National Congress was called in Karachi. In the same year, the youth organisation set up by Bhagat Singh also organised their conference in Karachi. Bose presided over that conference and said that Bhagat Singh was the symbol of the patriotic feeling and spirit which could be found in India during this time.

The spirit of patriotism was unbeatable but there was no change in the attitude of the government. He criticised the 'Gandhi-Irwin pact' but also said that the freedom fighters were in a struggling state and that's why they should not reject the present agreement. Rejecting this would mean equivalent to insulting Gandhiji.

CHAPTER 13
Bose's deteriorating health and escape to Europe

In the Karachi session Bose protested and spoke against the agreement. But later he gave his vote in favour of the pact. The other communists criticised his step. Bose also realised that he could not give any logical explanation for his actions.

Everybody knew that the round table conference was unsuccessful. On December 28, 1931 Gandhiji returned from England empty handed.

Meanwhile, during June to October there occurred two or three incidents of domination. In September, the jail authorities of Hizli camp fired on the prisoners without any reason while they were having their meal. Hearing about this incident Bose rushed to Hizli and brought their dead bodies to Kolkata. Rabindranath Tagore came to the Monument ground and criticised the government's action in front of a huge crowd.

On January 4, 1932, the Viceroy announced that the

duration of the ceasefire under the 'Gandhi-Irwin pact' was over. All over the country around 20,000 workers and leaders were immediately arrested. Bose was in Mumbai with Gandhiji when all this happened.

In January 1932, Bose was arrested and taken to Siwni jail. Facilities like electricity, etc. were not available in that prison. Due to this Bose soon fell ill. Around mid-April of that year his health severely deteriorated. The jail commissioner wrote to the Mumbai government requesting the transfer of Bose to some other prison where his health could be taken care of in a better manner. Bose was suffering from indigestion and backache as well at that time. The local doctors were of the opinion that he was suffering from T.B. Finally, Bose and his brother were transferred to the military hospital of Jabalpur. The doctors over there advised him to go to Chennai. The symptoms of T.B. could be clearly observed in him. He

was sent to the Bhuvali sanitorium, near Nainital. The stay in Bhuvali did not benefit him much and the government did not want him to die in prison because they knew that he was a beloved leader of the country and if he died, it would lead to terrible problems in India. The Government was also not interested in releasing him. Due to this they put forward a proposal to him to either go to Mumbai or Europe. Bose was prepared for this but he wanted to meet his parents before leaving. But the government was not ready to approve it and also put a condition that Bose would have to bear his own livelihood in Mumbai. But Bose was well aware of the consequences and realised that going independently to Europe would be the right decision.

CHAPTER 14
Bose's Educational Philosophy

Bose started his journey to Europe in order to restore his health. Fortunately the ship had originated from Italy and the people behaved properly with Bose. As he reached Venice, he encountered many journalists who were waiting for him. From there he went directly to Vienna. In Vienna, his room soon became the meeting point of many students of Indian origin. He was frequently visited by people from India.

The elder brother of Vallabhbhai Patel, Vitthalbhai Patel was very impressed with Bose and praised him a lot. When he was ill Bose was the one who took care of him and nursed him back to health. Bose was also near him when in October 1933, Patel died. Earlier, when Patel was not ill, Bose went on a trip for two months to Czechoslovakia, Poland and Germany.

The social revolution dreamt by Netaji was still a distant dream. A society of unaware illiterates was certainly less preferable than one of the aware illiterates, because very often illiterates display a greater humanity than self-announced educated people who only talk big.

Bose believed that education is an extremely important factor that contributes in the overall development of a

person. He dreamt of an independent India with educated citizens who would be well aware of their responsibilities and duties towards their country. He advocated basic education for all and higher education for the highly meritorious students. He believed that education will bring together the country and infuse a spirit of patriotism in the hearts of the people to participate in the freedom struggle and put an end to the foreign rule.

Thus, we may conclude that Bose was one of the leaders of national education. Though his name has not found its place in the history of national education in India alongside Tagore, Satish Chandra Mukherjee, Sri Aurobindo, etc. yet he was the first to give a real shape to national education.

CHAPTER 15
Originality of Thought

In a letter to the secretary of the Philosophical society of Scottish Church College on September 9, 1934, Bose wrote that, originality of thought was a priceless property of every human being. However, such qualities can grow only in an ideal environment. In an undated letter to Hari Charan Bagchi from Mandalay, Bose wrote that children should be allowed to taste the joy of creation at an early age. They should be encouraged to make something with their own hands, whether it be through clay modelling or tree-planting. The joy of such creation can never be left out.

Bose was of the view that manual training rather than memorisation of texts was necessary at the primary stage. This alone would make education a thing of joy rather than a thing of fear or burden for the children.

Netaji Bose would have found the modern tutorial homes totally pointless, since they waste all the talents of the students and turn them to puppets with parrot learning. He would have discouraged such an approach to learning that led to the conversion of lively students into boring automatons that have no ideas of their own and are just a part of the crowd.

Bose also advised teachers to take their students to the museum for teaching History and also use the globe and Atlas for teaching Geography. He believed that in order to make the process of education a successful endeavor, it was important that teachers are continuously trained and invent interesting methods to impart knowledge. Bose also laid stress on gardening, painting and drawing since he knew that without exposure to nature, it was impossible to mix children with trees and flowers.

Bose's guidelines for teachers are of long-lasting impacts that are relevant even today, particularly his view that a teacher must see everything from the student's point of view with love and sympathy. Otherwise he can never understand the difficulties of the student. The personality of the teacher was of the greatest importance and so was the method of teaching and the subject being taught.

In his speech delivered at the National Education Conference, Midnapore, on May 1923, Bose advised teachers to become awakened. They must become lively men who would encourage students to become courageous, truthful, patriotic and selfish by the example of their own character rather than through reading speeches, debates and quarreling reasons. He advised the use of experiments by teachers to simplify difficult things to dull students. He also advised to have textbooks written by knowledgeable men and also introduce a training scheme for teachers.

CHAPTER 16
End of Civil Disobedience

Tagore's Vishwa Bharati was an ideal role model for the educational institutes all over India. During his visit to Santiniketan, he made a remark on January 23, 1939 that, "a link between education and national ideals, which could not be found anywhere else, was seen there." Bose was not against accepting any worthy thing from the West. But he never wanted to accept anything at the cost of India's nationality. He was also a supporter of secular education.

Netaji's philosophy of education signified a positive view of life. In 1934, the Civil Disobedience Movement came to an end. At that time Jawaharlal Nehru was in jail like many other congressmen.

Bose gave a visa application to the British government for visiting the U.S.S.R., but he was rejected the visa. In 1936, Bose went to Berlin. Later that year he decided to go to Ireland, where he was invited by the government. During his stay in Europe, he felt that he was not being able to act freely. So he decided to come back to India.

Jawaharlal Nehru suggested that he should not come back at this moment but Bose was adamant.

On his return to India he was arrested by the police. His arrest was widely protested by his followers. First he was kept in the Mumbai jail and was later shifted to the Yerwada jail in Pune. He was not well and required treatment. So he was admitted to the Kolkata Medical

College on December 17, 1936. The demand for his release was continuously growing and he was finally released on March 17, 1937 without any condition. After this arrest he was supposed to take an active part in the political scenario immediately.

CHAPTER 17
The World Scene

After getting released, he was not able to give time to all the tasks assigned to him. The reason behind this was his health. He went to Dalhousie to take rest for six months but never lost touch with the current political situations as he kept reading the newspapers and magazines to keep him up-to-date.

He was not yet sure of the path he was to take and was disturbed due to this indecisiveness. On the world scene, Japan had attacked China. In India, under the leadership of Jawaharlal Nehru, there were concerned voices raised in China.

Bose returned to Kolkata during the beginning of October 1937. Nehru, who was the president of Congress at that time, was disturbed by the division of Congress in various groups and thought that Bose would be able to control this situation. Nehru was also disturbed due to the Muslim revolutionaries who considered 'Vande Matram' to be a Hindu song that did not make any reference to the diversified communities of the country. Bose was not in favour of making this song as a national song and understood that it was very important to provide a sense of belongingness to the Muslim community and not hurt their sentiments. Finally, a settlement was reached and the song 'Jana-Gana-Mana' was selected as our national anthem.

Bose took an active part in the meetings held in Kolkata. He was also elected as the mayor of Kolkata. Due to this kind of active participation he again fell ill and doctors advised him to go to Europe. This time Bose's stay was only for three months. He stayed in Austria where his health improved quickly. Here he wrote his autobiography, *An Indian Pilgrim*, but was not able to complete it.

At his request an Austrian woman, Emilie Schenkl came to live with him. They both knew each other since 1934 and were good friends. They ultimately fell in love

and later married each other. During his previous visit Bose never went to Britain, but this time he decided to go there. He reached London in January 1938. Hundreds of journalists were gathered there to meet him.

They asked him different types of questions and he replied to all of them in a very calm and composed manner. He expressed his opinion directly that if Britain gives independence to India and gives it the opportunity to make its own constitution then there would be very friendly relations between the two countries. In his short stay in Britain he met various big leaders of the labour party.

CHAPTER 18
Bose: The Congress President

This visit proved to be an important one as a local newspaper gave him the title of 'Indian De Valera.' In the year 1938, Bose was elected as the president of the 51st conference of Congress. However, Gandhiji didn't approve of this decision but there was no other choice for the post. Bose immediately came back to India and thus finished his trip. Now was the time when a new chapter of his life was going to begin. Gorden, the writer of his biography,

wrote that this was the period when he became a leader of the whole nation.

Bose was elected as the Congress President without any opposition in Haripura. This was just a formality. One of the groups of Congress, which belonged to the southern region, was uncertain about Bose. Bose in his Presidential address said, "We people, who have become the slaves of the British Empire and are fighting for our as well other country's cause, are luckily fighting for economic liberation of British people."

Thereafter, he raised the question about the role of labour unions and farmers. Bose stated his opinion about the union of the labourers and farmers into the congress to fight against the British. He also said that they will have to face worst conditions in order to get freedom from the British rule. Congress was at that time the largest institution for public protest.

The Leftist on the whole accepted his speech in general but was shocked at one point. On the issue of the foreign policy, there was no strong criticism of Germany, Italy or Japan in his speech. Nehru and the Communists did not like this idea. Bose said that only these countries could help them in fighting against the British no matter what were the internal policies of these countries.

As the Congress President, Bose had proposed one single language for the whole nation. He wanted one national language, a mixture of Hindi and Urdu, a language that was termed as 'Hindustani'. In this conference there was no open fight between Bose and other Congress members.

CHAPTER 19
Period of Struggle and Escape

Nehru and Bose were the only two leftist (supporter of social change and non-religious) leaders in the Congress Working Committee. Bose was not in favour of any type of communalism (group action) and he basically supported secularism (non religious). Bose more or less agreed with the congress leadership on Hindu-Muslim relations.

The conference of All India Congress Committee was held on April 29, 1939, in Kolkata. In that Conference Bose resigned from the post of President.

On May 3, Bose formed a new party within the congress. He gave it the name - 'Forward Bloc'. The 'Forward Bloc' was based on Bose's own military rules. It readily addressed his revolutionary ideas and he used to openly speak against the Congress. He said that the Congress dictator was same as Hitler.

A new phase in his life had started. The cruelties of the British were increasing day by day. Bose decided to celebrate July 9, 1939 as the 'leftist day'. The top leaders of

the congress requested the people not to take part in this celebration. They also declared Bose as unfit for the post of the Bengal Congress Committee. Bose in his speech on 19th August said that the punishment that he was given will not affect him but will affect thousands of Indians.

Rabindranath Tagore normally kept out of the political fight but this time he also supported Bose. Now there was a direct conflict between Gandhiji and Bose. The time had come for both to take two different paths.

In September 1939, World War II started. The congress announced that it would not help the British in the war until and unless the British government promises that after this war India would get independence. In June 1940, Bose went to Vardha to meet Gandhiji and reached a conclusion that they would never agree with each other. Bose returned to Kolkata and started a protest in order to remove the statue of Hallwell. But the government arrested him a day earlier under the Indian Safety Law.

Bose was arrested and was sent to jail for an unknown period. Bose decided to flee from jail and go abroad. In order to accomplish this task, he started a hunger strike. Within one week he became too weak and on December 5, 1940, he was released from jail.

CHAPTER 20
Plan of Escape

Bose made a contact with Akbar Shah after his release. Akbar Shah was the main culprit of Bolshevik conspiracy ten years ago. Akbar had come to Kolkata. There he made a plan of escape with Bose. Their plan was that they would go to Afghanistan first and then with the help of Kisaan party's Achar Singh Cheema they would move further.

On January 16, Bose disguised himself as a Muslim and went to Gomo with his nephew Shishir to Shishir's

elder brother, Ashok's home. The next day both the brothers took Bose to the Gomo station and Bose boarded the Kalki Mail. After he arrived in Delhi, he changed the train and boarded the Frontier Mail to go to Peshawar. Akbar Shah was also on that train and Bose got down at the Cantonment station. He then went to a safe place with Akbar Shah.

On January 21, Bhagat Ram Talwar met Bose and made a detailed plan about going to Afghanistan.

On January 27, 1941, Bose and Bhagat Ram reached Kabul. Recent research shows that the British secret agency knew about this earlier but they did not act because they wanted him to remain out of the country.

They found the address of the German embassy on 2nd February and talked to the German authorities. In mid-February one of the employees of German Embassy, Thomas, told Bhagat Ram that Germany, Italy and Japan had collectively told U.S.S.R to give Bose a transit visa. At the end of February, Bose made a fake passport in Italy in disguise as Mohammed Ziauddin. In March, a car picked Bose from his house and entered Russia. He then boarded a train, which took him to Moscow. From there he went to Berlin by air. He wanted Germany's help in the Indian freedom struggle and wanted to form an army from the Indian prisoners of war. Now the plan of Bose to free India took a new turn in Germany.

To know how the INA took birth after the British military defeat, in the Malaya-Singapore theatre in

December 1941, a long forgotten chapter in the Indian freedom struggle needs to be recalled.

The British army after a try, broke the British Indian Army cantonments in 1915 and then many Ghadar leaders of Punjab and Bengal revolutionaries were executed or sentenced to live in jail for a long time by the British government.

CHAPTER 21
Azad Hind Fauj

Many Ghadar leaders and Bengal revolutionaries, who escaped the British hold, ran from India and took shelter in countries like Thailand. Rash Behari Bose, who planned the revolt in the British Indian Army in the year 1915, received shelter in Japan, although Japan was friendly with Britain after the 1914-18 war with Germany.

Among the revolutionaries living in Thailand in 1941, there were two very remarkable persons. Gyani Pritam Singh, a Sikh missionary was living in Thailand since 1933 after the end of the Civil Disobedience movement in India. Another was Swami Satyananda Puri, a former Anusheelan revolutionary in Bengal, who taught Oriental philosophy in Calcutta University and also at Rabindranath Tagore's Shantiniketan.

Japan planned to rage a war against the Western powers in Asia but they did not include India in it because they planned to help India to fight against the British rule. After becoming victorious the Japanese troupes asked the

Indian troops to surrender and this marked the formation of the Indian National Army.

In February 1943 at Singapore's Farrer Park, nearly 50,000 troops - defeated and demoralised Indian troops, NCOs and officers - had gathered for formal surrender. Lt. Col. Hunt, on behalf of Lt. Gen. A E Percival, the General Official-Command of the British forces, formally handed over the Indians to the Japanese command. The Japanese separated the Indians from the whites.

Thus, Major Fujiwara, Gyani Pritam Singh, Capt. Mohan Singh and Capt. Mohammad Akram of the 1st Battalion, appeared together at Farrer Park.

After Col. Hunt's formal surrender, Fujiwara spoke of Indians as brothers and fellow-Asians, who had long suffered the white man's dominance and racial difference.

Thereafter, Capt. Mohan Singh encouraged the defeated crowd with a speech and asked them to join a force for the freedom of their motherland.

He told them that instead of fighting as a part of Britain's army to keep other Asians in dominance, Indians must form their own nationalist army which would cooperate with Japan to end British rule in their own motherland, India. This began the formal effort to organise the Indian National Army.

CHAPTER 22
Bose: The INA Chief

Gyani Pritam Singh spoke about the rise of freedom struggle in India and said that he would lead the independence movement in India. The speeches made by Fujiwara, Mohan Singh and Pritam Singh, lifted the defeated groups to think something positive and inspired them to fight for the independence of their country.

The Indian National Army took birth in the minds of the surrendered soldiers on the night of February 17-18, 1942 at Farrer Park in Singapore.

Among the first group of Indian officers who accepted the INA concept were Capt. Mohan Singh, Capt. Habibur Rahman Khan, Capt. Ehsan Qadir, Capt. Talib Din, Capt. Mahboob Ahmed, Capt. Ram Sarup and Capt. Gurbaksh Singh Dhillon.

Bose took command of the INA on July 4, 1943. His very presence brought new life and zeal into the broken force. All gaps in the INA disappeared. The reunion turned the INA into a fighting force.

❖ Subhash Chandra Bose ❖

By October 21, 1943, the Provisional Government of Azad Hind had been announced and the INA was already in the battlefront disturbing the British forces who were trying to get hold of Burma by the sea-route and make Akyab the beach head. The INA fought very well in the Arakans forcing the British force to fall back, leaving a vast quantity of small and heavy weapons. By December 1943, the 1st Division of the INA, commanded by Col. Mohammad Zaman Kiani, moved to Rangoon. Netaji Subhash Chandra Bose's army moved the headquarters from Singapore to Rangoon. According to Japan's plan, an expedition was launched to capture Assam in order to break the routes of American supplies to Chiang Kai-Shek's Army and also form a friendly relationship with Burma from the Indian side.

CHAPTER 23
Victory and Defeat of INA

Many INA officials sent by sea and land routes to India were captured by the British.

The Japanese agency suspected British elements among the Indian prisoners of war for these losses. Japan was shocked to know that though Anglo-American spy network worked in Asia, the British and Americans had been able to break the secret code.

Hideki Tojo was the general of the Imperial Japanese Army who was assigned the task of helping Bose's Army against the British Raj. After meeting Bose for the first time on June 14, 1943, Tojo was deeply impressed by Bose's intelligence of the war situation and his leadership capability. He had never met an Indian of Bose's standard before.

On April 18, 1944, the suicide force of the INA commander Col. Shaukat Malik broke through the British defense system and captured Moirang in Manipur. It was an emotional occasion for the INA men. Col. Shaukat Malik unfolded the tricolour Indian national flag in Moirang and the INA progressed towards Imphal. The Azad Hind administration took control of the freed Indian territory.

In August 1945, Bose boarded a Japanese military plane to travel from Singapore to Japan. But, somewhere over Formosa his plane crashed and Bose was announced dead.

Since then, many theories were made about his disappearance, like he remained in exile, another theory said that he was captured by the Russian army and more recently yet another theory has evolved that maintains that he survived for a few days but ultimately died and was cremated in Japan etc.

Thus, ended the life of a revolutionary leader of India, whose ideas are still alive in the minds of people who have a passionate love and unending patriotism for their country.

CHAPTER 24
Bose's Life Events in Chronology

- Jan 23, 1897 - Subhash Chandra Bose was born in Bengal
- 1913 - Bose joined the Presidency College in Calcutta
- 1914 - Went to Northern India, looking for a spiritual master to show him the right path
- Feb l916 - Bose was expelled from the college
- July 1917 - Bose was re-admitted to the college
- 1918- He joined the University Training Corps
- 1919 - He got first class honours in philosophy and went to England
- 1920 - Bose passed the Civil Service open examination and held the fourth rank
- Jan 1921 - Bose offered to work at the Congress National College in Calcutta
- Apr 1921 - Bose resigned from the Indian Civil Service
- July 1921 - Bose returned to India
- 1921 - Subhash Chandra Bose entered Indian politics

- 1921 - Bose organized a boycott of the Prince of Wales' visit to India.
- Dec 10, 1921 - Bose was arrested for parading illegally
- 1922 - Bose spent six weeks, working in the flooded regions of Northern Bengal
- Oct 1924 - Bose was arrested as a suspected dangerous terrorist
- Jan 1925 - Bose was removed from Alipore jail to the great fort of Mandalay in Burma
- 1926 - Bose was nominated as a candidate for Bengal Legislative Assembly
- May 16, 1927 - He was released from the jail
- Dec 1927 - Bose became the General Secretary of the Congress
- 1928 - Bose commanded the parade of Congress Volunteers' at the Congress Assembly
- Jan 23, 1930 - Bose was arrested for leading an independent procession
- July 1930 - He staged a hunger strike against the prison treatment
- Sep 25, 1930 - He was released from prison and was elected the Mayor of Calcutta
- 1931 - Bose was arrested for visiting the disturbed area of Bengal
- Jan 2, 1932 - He was arrested again

- Feb 22, 1932 - Bose was released on the condition that he would leave for Europe
- May, 1932- Issued a manifesto in Vienna.
- Nov 1934 - Bose released a book, *The Indian Struggle*
- 1934- Bose flew to India
- 1938-1939 - Elected President of the Indian National Congress. Rabindranath Tagore felicitated Bose as 'Desh-Nayak'
- Jan 17, 1941 - Bose escaped from house arrest in India and fled secretly to Berlin
- Jan 26, 1943 - He celebrated 'Independence Day' in Berlin
- July 2, 1943 - Bose reached Singapore
- July 1943 - Announced Azad Hind Government in Singapore
- Aug 25, 1943 - Bose took charge of the Indian National Army
- Dec 1943 - 2nd division of INA was formed
- 1944 - Bose lost Imphal Campaign
- 1945 - Believed to have died in an airplane crash.

www.ingramcontent.com/pod-product-compliance
Lightning Source LLC
LaVergne TN
LVHW091317080426
835510LV00007B/530